Words From The River

2nd Edition

MALIK S. CANTY

aka Word Bird

Words From The River, 2nd Edition

Copyright © 2018 Malik S. Canty

Published by Inspired 4 U Publications,
an imprint of Inspired 4 U Ministries, LLC

http://inspired4upublications.com

Published June 2018

ISBN-10: 0999425226
ISBN-13: 978-0999425220

DEDICATION

To My Children:

I have not always represented my words, but they have represented me, so you knew my heart.

Continue to be the waters for my soul because you have loved me, instead of judged me, during my spiritual darkness days and when my life was like a turbulent river...

My misuse of time didn't become a crime, and I am still standing, still creating, and still being lifted whenever I am in your presence.

Like the river, all the waters are not rough and our love was strong enough to always keep us in touch with each other...

May the Ancestors and the Creator continue to bless and watch over everything you love and everyone you touch.

I smile at the future because you are my representatives.

Listen carefully to the Waters of Knowledge
for its Wisdom Didn't Come From College.

– Word Bird

CONTENTS

I Write to open the eyes
of those whose Minds Remain Blind.

– Word Bird

FOREWORD

Since his coming to join in fellowship with us at St. Paul Community Baptist Church, Malik Samuel Canty has been both a life source and a life force. His poetry promotes both calm and restlessness. I dub him prophetic in his poetry.

What an honor it is to write this introduction. Dr. C.A.W Clark of the Good Street Church in Dallas, Texas has said that "a man who needs a long introduction does not deserve it and a man that deserves a long introduction does not need it."

Malik Canty deserves a long introduction and via the books content, he introduces himself.

Malik Canty is Poet Laureate of St. Paul Community Baptist Church and whenever he speaks, even like E. F. Hutton, we listen.

Ladies and Gentlemen, Brothers and Sisters, Friends:

Malik Samuel Canty – " The Word Bird".

There is a verse in the Scriptures, in the Old Testament, that tells us: "Wherever the river flows, all shall live."

Drink deep, my people, drink deep.

— *Rev. Dr. Johnny Ray Youngblood, May 2006*
Pastor of Mt. Pisgah Baptist Church
Pastor Emeritus of St. Paul Community Baptist Church.

These words tell the stories about the continued struggle of our people; and like the River, we keep flowing and we keep going.

– Word Bird

WORDS FROM THE RIVER

Out of the depths of antiquity, the flow of stories passed through the rivers... Langston spoke of them, Maya was a student of them, Jesus walked on them... I learned from the likes of them.

Come into the waters of my soul... Read what the spirits have revealed to an ear that hears.

An endless stream of thoughts flows through my pen as the tearful waters of humanity is stored on the river banks...

Journey with me on a mental ship, as we ride the tide of life through the Spoken Words that my soul heard...

Every note is a story, "Words From The River" came from the depths of ancestral grief, modern grief, and from those who feel they have no power when they speak...

I Speak for Them... I Write for Them...

The River is Timeless, Ageless, a Natural Wonder...

Every Now and Then, it speaks to the Lost Children of Antiquity...

Listen carefully to the Waters of Knowledge for its Wisdom Didn't Come From College.

I WRITE

I Write to uplift your spirit...

I Write to open the eyes of those whose Minds Remain Blind...

I Write to confront Racism, Sexism, Color-Bashing, and to reach the heart of the ASSASSINS....

I-Write-Because-You-Won't...

I Write because it is a Gift and I Must Share It...

I Write because of people like you, unspoken voices, can't take time to write it down people, Unconcerned People.

I Write because I love to see the expressions on your face when my words penetrate denial and smack historical lies back into their tombs...

When My Words Hug you with the Reality of Truth as you shake your head in agreement...

I Write because the pain I see on a daily basis is affecting All the Races...

I-Write-Because-You-Won't.

MANHOOD

Spiritually sound and profound, everyone knows when Pastor Johnny Ray Youngblood is around.

In his walk, in his talk, he stands out before he even opens his mouth.

He speaks in the language that draws men unto him... Speaks with a fire that commands respect.

His presence, his reverence and knowledge of the Word of God has made many clamor to hear his teaching and preaching.

Manhood is put on full display when you witness the walk and talk of Johnny Ray.

Dignified, Brilliant, a Religious Giant who Exemplifies Black Manhood that would have made Malcolm smile at his fiery style.

Many in the status quo know that he is nobody's Negro...

He is a Builder of men, a Warrior for God, and a Preacher who speaks in the language of men.

Black and Proud he often boasts, not afraid to tackle and prove that racism is not a ghost.

Manhood Teacher and One Hell-of-a Preacher... Dr. Johnny Ray Youngblood.

Warrior in and out the pulpit...

Strength and Strong convictions can be clearly seen from this Black King...

Manhood... In His Walk, in His Talk...

Feared and Revered no matter where he appears.

Pastor Dr. Johnny Ray Youngblood: The Warrior Preacher.

LIGHTS

Every step, every misstep, were Teaching Tools...

Ordinary people go through ordinary things, Not the Blessed...

I see a Light in you that never seems to dim...

Malcolm had that Light: Powerful and Serene....

A Light that wasn't always there, but came through trials and acceptance that God is in Charge of Your Life...

Every Conversation with you is a Buffet of Wisdom...

Those Lights attract, attack, soothe, and teach those who are blessed to see it, and especially those who refuse to believe it...

God-Given-Lights... Saturated in Concern and Love...

It's all around you... I have felt its pull as they clamor for your Teaching and Preaching...

Fiery... Truthful... God-Given-Lights.

Shaka had that Light in his Spear, Nat had it in his Fury... Harriet's Light gave her Night Eyes through the swamps and woods...

Dr. King is a product of the Light. Elijah was taught by the Light, Jesus came out of the Light…

I see that Light in You, Haters do too…

Tried to take your Light, Deny the existence of your Light…

The Light is in your Face; Illuminating with a glow that grows…

Generated from within, the Light is God Smiling in Your Direction.

Your Light has Power and it permeates your Words so that others are captivated by your speech, motivated and stimulated by your teaching…

Many fear you, many adore you, none can stop you…

He who has been enlightened most often frightens those who profess love of truth when deception is their mate…

Keep teaching, keep preaching, and keep reaching the mind!

PRESENCE

There is Power in Your Color...

The Moment you walk into any place, any room, any area, there is a Change in the air...

People notice you even when you don't seek spotlight, Your Presence stirs emotions...

I have seen it in the eyes of those who resent and feel threatened by Your Presence...

Seen it in the eyes of those who need and understand the value of Your Presence...

You can Change an atmosphere when you appear...

By accident or on purpose, when you surface, people take notice...

When you March in volumes, there is fear in certain sects that you want more than just respect and that is something certain groups refuse to accept.

Your Presence can stir a lot of positive and negative emotions, bring worry to a culture that only sought your destruction...

Your Presence throughout history has been subjected to all kinds of physical and mental abuse, by other men who sought to subjugate and enslave you...

They seem to hear the fire of Malcolm when you

speak...

They act like a Million Men walk beside you, as you enter into places where they feel you don't belong.

Watch the eyes, feel the body language, see the anguish and the fears gather strength, as you come closer into view...

Your Presence is the Reason for The Killing Seasons of Men of Color...

Continue to Rise, Continue to Change the air when you appear; You are the descendants of the Original Man and Great Civilizations, started with people who look like you...

Step out the shadows; Children need to see the Real You, The World needs to see the Real you, and you need to be the Real You!

A FATHER'S STORY

I have and will always be there for you, My Son...

Our separation from each other has a painful history that is bigger than Me or your Mother.

Bigger and calculated so that you would never look to me for Strength.

I knew I could have done more to fight the "Willie Lynch" method of planned separation of the Blackman from his family.

I need you to hear the tears of my words and grow from them...

Life is a series of events and things happen that we can't control or prevent sometimes...

The trials don't come with an expiration date...

You Must Be Strong!

Show them what you are made of... Show them that, no matter what, you will not be stopped because you come from Divine Stock...

Let go of the anger and let go of those emotions that unleash frustration and stress in your Powerful Mind.

Our Separation has a history... Our future together is up to us...

The Missing years of my life in your life came with a price, which I am still paying for…

Blame is all around and I accept wearing the crown as the king culprit for your lack of emotions towards me…

When you reached out, No Where to Be Found Became My New Name.

When the growing pains needed a voice, I was never your first choice…

Missed so much because I couldn't handle my own stuff…

So many men like myself are in need of releasing the reasons for the Running Away, Staying Away, and not being Confident and Strong enough to be there for their children…

May these words reach their eyes and their pride…

May these words touch their hardened hearts and make them seek their children's forgiveness.

Seek their children before their health deteriorates and their body starts to betray them with permission from Father Time…

Our children are our future no matter what we did in the past…

May these words be a doorway to the heart of a child in search of answers, and for Fathers who continue to be missing in the life of their seeds…

This is a Father's Story, confession is food for the soul.

BETRAYAL

I saw it in your eyes and it hurt me...

How could you? Why would you?

Dupe me, double cross me, betray me?

I guess maybe I am a bit too sensitive, after all Judas had to have descendants too, I just never thought one would be you...

Thirty pieces used to be the going rate... What did it take to get you to betray the trust, the bond, and the kindness that I always had reserved for you?

I saw it in your eyes, it's too late to deny, and I only want to know why?

Betrayal has inflicted and impeded the progress of Nations, it is Satan's most powerful weapon...

When it hits home, you know the devil is on the roam.

I saw its shadow in your eyes, all I want to know is why?

ANCIENT WARRIOR

I am an Ancient Warrior, a soldier of a glorious past...

My battles have been many... I am fearless, been summoned many times to do battles in many places.

My battle gear is made from the elements of tears.

My Weapons have changed with the time; I am always ready and steady.

I do not get much rest for I am always on alert.

I am an Ancient Warrior...

I fought with the Mau-Mau, I stood with Shaka, I marched with Hannibal, and I tutored Malcolm, Angela, and Huey.

I showed Harriet the need for staying and operating underground.

Wherever Injustice is to be found, you will find me.

The Weak and Oppressed don't let me sleep, for their anguish and pain has kept the dust from settling on my tomb.

All the other Ancient Warriors that came before me have made a spiritual alliance with me.

My endurance comes from a Divine Source that many people thought was lost.

I am an Ancient Warrior; I cried at Calvary, for my
teacher had ascended and I could not come because
my work here was not done.

Modern Grief keeps the peace of sleep from me, so I
keep my battle gear on until another Savior is born.

I am a sentry who has been here for centuries.

Stolen Legacy, Racism and the abuse of the Dark
Continent kept me strong and anticipating another
call to do battle.

I mount the wind, I ride the tides, many have tried to
kill me, but I cannot die.

Strong like a petrified tree, the blood of countless
generations flow through me.

I cannot rest, I will never fully sleep, and the bodies
that make up the Middle Passage floors are always
calling out to me to set their Restless spirits free.

I am an Ancient Warrior...

Abner Louima's Screams interrupted my dreams and
brought me back to the present.

I weep each time a leader dies and a child cries.

I am an Ancient Warrior; wherever you find injustice,
you will find elements of me.

DOORWAYS

The Doorway of Knowledge has opened a little more...

Hidden Ancestral Secrets are being brought to the surface of consciousness...

Exploration of Time and Space has intensified...

For all the progress made in Modern Times, we are still far behind the Ancestral Minds that were here in the beginning...

Untapped Doorways located in our mind have yet to be opened...

Our Ancestors tried to Instill the Gift of True Knowledge to us, but Ignorance Closed the Door...

Science for all that it has discovered, still has no idea of the Power, of the Wisdom, that is located all around us and inside of us...

The Ancient were not Pleasure Seekers, they were Guardians who sought to Protect and Maintain Civilization in its Grandeur...

Meditations, Spiritual Realization, can only enhance Your Mind...

Find the Power Center in Your Mind, tap into it if you can... The Ancient with their agreement with Father Time are waiting to guide you and protect you...

For Centuries, the Ancestors have allowed many people to treat their beliefs, their gifts to the world, as obsolete antiquities...

Tears on the Pyramids, a Weeping Sphinx, Blood on the Moon, and the Realm of the Spirits are sending new messages on Earth and in Space...

The Doorway of Knowledge will only open to those who have a Spiritual Key, and to those who deal with Reality....

BLACKMAN

It was You, Blackman, who First named the Stars... Built Cities and Monuments as a testimony of your innate Creative Powers.

It was You, who started civilization on its path, brought the Different Tribes of the World Together.

Blackman, your magnificent mind could never be enslaved for long periods of Time.

Blackman, You with your Gifted Building Hands, have played a significant role in the Birth of Nations.

Blackman, Slavery could not stop you, Racism could not stop you, and only You can stop You from returning to Greatness.

Blackman, the Ancestors are relying and waiting on you to Find your True Self and show the world that you were Born To Lead.

Waiting on You to permanently remove the Mind Shackles that have served to hinder your growth, blind your vision, and keep you full of indecision.

So much you have forgotten Blackman... So much...

The world will continue to look at you as 3/5 of a man as long as you, Run from responsibility, run from commitment, Run from True Knowledge of Self.

Blackman, has the Fire in your soul been quenched?

Return to Greatness Blackman...

Return to Greatness!

THE APOLOGY

I am sorry Black Woman, for not being your king in times of need...

Sorry for running away from my responsibilities when you needed me most...

I know I have taken flight, instead of standing and fighting for the preservation of my family...

This society has always treated me like damaged goods, I didn't need you to see or treat me that way too...

I am sorry Black Woman, for the countless tears I heaped upon you...

I am sorry Black Woman, for the cheating and mistreatments, and the non-Communications of my fears...

I know that you have carried the burden on your firm, yet gentle, shoulders of raising our children by yourself with very little help from me...

I am sorry for being afraid of commitment...

I am sorry for making myself believe that you can fulfill all my needs when even I can't...

I am sorry, so I apologize to you for not being able to handle the residue of slavery, the 3/5 amendments, the stripping of my soul by those who still seek to break me…

I apologize for not trusting anyone, not confiding in anyone, not truly loving anyone, including myself…

I am sorry that somewhere along the lines, I forgot to treasure you…

You have always been a rock, no matter how much others have tried to wear you out or tear you down…

I am sorry that the only legacy I left behind in our relationship was tears…

I am sorry it took me so long to realize that fighting with you is more productive than fighting against you…

Please accept this apology from a Black Man who has finally got in touch with his True Feelings, and may this apology clear up a myth that Men don't care about Sh...

ASK YOURSELF

How can we Rise in Positive Numbers if some of us keep finding excuses to not elevate ourselves when given the chance?

How can we Compete with those others, who scorn us, mock our intelligence, ridicule our schools as inferior, spread lies and half-truths about our Magnificent and Rich Heritage?

Ask Yourself... How can I get my Latino brothers, Native American brothers, Black brothers to realize that We All are extensions of the African Mystique?

What methods will work to open the eyes and minds of those of us who are blind in vision and see Only the Beauty of Self and no other races?

Ask Yourself... How can I stop the inherent denial of so many people of Color without getting into an argument and watching denial strengthen itself with Anger as Truth gets Twisted?

How can we Rise In Positive Numbers when human chameleons prance around bragging about things that are irrelevant, like hair texture, color of skin, mocking the language of a kin they pretend is not related to them?

Ask Yourself... How can we get stronger as a people when some of our neighborhoods are infested with drugs, crime, and everybody shows indifference?

Sometimes it only takes One Individual to Stand Up and Lead The Way...

One Individual to show by example, by commitment, dedication and a fire that stirs the masses into action, stir a City, a Town and sometimes a Nation...

Ask Yourself: Am I The One?

13

MENTAL DEATH

It makes the Mind Sleep, yet you Try it, Buy it, and Lie about it.

It makes the Mind Sleep, yet you claimed that it helps release chains on the unused parts of your brain.

False energy, heightened awareness, powerful inner thoughts that you have been deceived and made to believe, comes from its mind-altering-contents.

It makes the Mind Sleep, takes you to places that are full of danger, filled with others who also hear its seductive, self-destructive voice calling them.

It makes the Mind Sleep so that they fall in love with a False God who promotes medication of thoughts and dreams, as a solution for things they can't accept or change.

It makes the Mind Sleep... What's in a name, so many names, so many victims, willing to throw their life away for another Hit, another Pill, another Drink, Another Needle, another Smoke...

It makes the Mind Sleep Taking away from your natural creative juices and replacing them with so many illusions that only enhance your confusion.

Stagnating your growth and putting all your hopes in a bottle, while giving birth to the seeds of procrastination.

It makes the Mind Sleep, so many names, so many masks, each one promising some type of Mental Blast, when all they really want to do is kill-your-as*.

It makes the Mind Sleep, Beware of its Many Forms!

FOR A REASON

There are certain people destined to cross your path.

Sent to you for reasons known only to Our Creator...

Sent to alter your thinking, your beliefs, and sometimes your Heart...

Sent to ease some of your negative digestions that may be stalling your Growth.

Crossing your path, entering into your life at the right Time, bringing much needed relief to your sometimes troubled mind...

Coming at you with words or deeds that remind you of your existence, remind you that you still got it going on strong...

Making you smile whenever your paths cross, lifting up your spirit, relaxing your soul and mind at the same time.

Though life is filled with trials and tribulations and people are constantly stopping and going out of your life, every now and then Someone Special will cross your path...

Making you see the value of you, even if you are feeling down and blue with stress weighing heavily on you...

At the right moment, someone will be sent in Your Path, taking away Mental pain, telling you about the Benefits of Accepting Change...

Lifting you from your personal worries for a moment, for a second, just so that you can smile again, feel good about yourself again...

Don't give Haters, Fools, Insecure People any of your strength, none of your time, because happiness will become an illusion, which will keep you saturated in stress and confusion.

For a reason, these words found you; God is not the only one who saw something Special in You...

When all is said and done, I expect to see you glowing like the Sun because you finally found that Special Someone!

HURRICANE SANDY

Scientist called SANDY a Monster and predicted that her forces would be so intense that the Northern Coast would shake and her waters would be unprecedented.

Shut down Mass Transit, Shut down Major Airports, Evacuate and Shut down the roads, the streets, load up on supplies and get ready for her mighty tides.

SANDY made them close the schools, close the businesses, stop and think, because everything around could be drowned and never again found.

SANDY made them shop until the shelves were empty.

SANDY stopped the Playoffs and the payoffs that were forced to yield to Her God Given Power.

Forced to watch the awesome sight, as her waters merged with other bodies of water to allow the beholders to witness Her God Given Power.

Massive waves of biblical proportion raged towards the shores... Clearing the bridges, clearing the beach houses, and those houses that dared to stay occupied and challenge Her Fury.

Her Winds Roared and buildings shook, trees became airborne and tossed like twigs, landing on houses, on cars, and on people.

SANDY, is she the one the Scriptures foretold? Is she the one sent to remind them that no man-made-preparations can withstand the Will of God?

No hiding places or impenetrable fortresses built by man can be out of view or brought down, unless it's the Will of God.

On their knees went the faithful, flocking to Churches, Temples, and Mosques, seeking Spiritual Shelter and Divine Protection.

It was written "Every Knee Would Bow."

SANDY got the attention of our Scientists, our computers and Satellites, Her powerful display left many in Awe at what they saw...

Evacuate everyone in her path, secure the shores, check all Levees and hope they stay steady.

Slowly feed the public information, assure them not to panic; while behind secret doors, the selected few are already relocated, already secured and think they can hide from the Will of God or the Cleansing of God.

SANDY made the waters unify to remind them who has the Real Power.

Her Presence will linger long after She is gone...
Her Devastations will be etched in our memories...

Every tunnel took a hit, every bridge took a hit, Cities and States will cringe, and thank their Creator for just being a witness and not a victim of SANDY.

Pray that her Kin stay away. Pray that their waters and their winds are not angrier than she was.

In the cocoon is where you wait and anticipate
a better day, better health, renewal of strength.

– Word Bird

COCOON

I Have Watched You Look at Yourself with One
Eye...

An Eye that doesn't give you the credit that
someone so beautiful as you deserve.

An Eye that is filled with immense pride,
but still feel empty inside...

You are the most unassuming flower I have ever
seen, surely you are a Queen.

Your modesty is to be commended, capturing a
Rare Treasure, like you, is highly recommended.

You Are Going Through A Stage...

A stage where the Real you is Hidden
by the Worried you.

A stage that is the beginning stage for your
Rebirth from Previous hurts.

I have seen you wrap yourself tightly in your
cocoon... Peeping out occasionally, hoping
no one sees your Private Misery.

I have seen you try to hide the tears
from your sensitive eyes, as you battle
for control of your health.

I look forward towards your Coming-Out-Party, where the flower within gets a chance to shine again.

Get a chance to strut your stuff for your Time Has Come...

In the cocoon is where you wait and anticipate a better day, better health, renewal of strength.

Wait until you shed the dead skin and start living again.

As you wait, don't lose faith...

Your day is coming and I want to be one of the first to congratulate you on your new attitude, new strength, new confidence...

In the Cocoon, Is Where You Now Reside...

Soon, You Will No Longer Have To Hide.

THEIR EYES NO LONGER HAD FIRE

Their Eyes No Longer Had Fire In Them...

Vacant, empty, defeated was the dominant expressions on the faces of the men.

Angry, despondent, no lights, no life could be clearly seen as they moved, as if driven by unseen hands that choke them with every step.

Voiceless warriors, loveable zombies, street casualties, living while dead...

Venom flowing out their lips, snarling at the life they live, and angry about some of the things they did.

The heat of life is like an unwanted Sun that they want no part of.

Their Eyes No Longer Had Fire...

Nothing to live for, no one to love, don't believe there is no GOD up above... Body language, clothing, all reek with defeat.

Black faces, White faces, Brown faces all showing traces of agony... All showing signs that they have given up and accepted their fate.

I have seen them moving aimlessly to and from, with eyes that don't believe GOD had a Son.

These men, who walk the streets, ride the subways, roaming without purpose, cursing, hurting, never certain where they will eat, where they will sleep, are still GOD'S Lost Sheep...

Pray for them, pray for the men whose very presence makes you feel uncomfortable. Their Eyes No Longer Have Fire, and Living is something Many of Them No Longer Desire.

EBONY FLOWERS

My Ebony Flowers, so Tender, so, shy, and so willing to hide the Natural Beauty you have inside...

The Garden of Life has many flowers, out of all the rest, you always show attributes of being one-of the-best...

My Ebony Flowers, please don't stifle your glow or let others stop you from trying to grow...

Full Lips, Rich thick hair, Black Skin, Brown skin, Fair skin, everything about you can make men drool and act like fools, just to get your attention...

Continue to light up a room when you enter, continue to be the model of beauty and strength, elegance and class, that others secretly and openly envy and try to emulate...

My Ebony Flowers, you have glowing power that is both captivating and alluring...

When you make up your mind to shine, smiling eyes and faces follow your every step...

Your DNA, Divine-Natural-Aura, is Second to None...

Mother of Civilization, Goddess, and The First Queen, are titles that originated from you Black Woman...

My Ebony Flowers, your beauty is rich like the Nile, you never have to emulate someone else's style...

Your Color is like no others...

Your Touch can make an Angel Blush...

My Ebony Flowers, no matter your Shape, Height, Weight, You are the Model to follow...

When all is said and done, Your Glow is the Only One that can compete with the Sun!

19

ANGER

Our Anger towards each other has been well orchestrated...

Our Bitterness keeps showing itself in many forms...

The inside wars in some of our neighborhoods have gone on too long...

The Dope, the Coke, the Seductive and Destructive Smoke, the Liquor, the Forties, and the Lost Humans hooked on Heroin and Crack, have increased along with the death count...

The Weeping mothers, the attacks on each other over trivial matters, only show how we have lost the love for each other as a people...

The mis-trust among us is like a fungus that won't leave us...

Our Anger is like a raging uncontrollable hurricane that will land and destroy everything in its path...

Your disappointments are shared openly and secretly; your tears, which you show on the inside and outside, have a river of companions.

We, as People of Color, have too many murals of young men decorating and reminding us of our Dying Neighborhoods...

We have too many fights and disagreements, and not

enough unity...

The Great African Tree grows weak for her lost roots, who have forgotten and been taught how to Forget her...

Our Anger has to stop being unleashed on Each other...

Where has the love, we should have for each other, gone?

On contact, we sometimes have a problem with each other...

On contact, it was embedded for generations to not trust and respect each other...

The wrong stare has led to confrontations, the Wrong Colors of clothes have led to violence between our youth...

Our Elders walk in fear around home, our children can no longer play safely in the parks...

Our Anger has to be harnessed or the daily eruptions and destructions that some of us do to each other will continue, until We Are No More...

Stop the Violence! Make it More Than Just Words, and please don't ever panic because you are the descendants of the First People On The Planet...

Now is the Time, Not Yesterday;

Now is the Time!

20

MIDDLE EAST

It is the Cradle of three of the World's Greatest Religions: Judaism, Christianity, Islam.

Middle East, can't find Peace, can't let the Prophets rest while Death and Destruction keep getting fed...

The Wars have taken place on Holy Grounds.

Precious Blood, of the innocent, of the angry, saturate the soil.

In a place where the Prophets walk, a battle rages throughout the land...

Centuries old battles between different religious sects, each demanding respect for their beliefs, and for their Prophets...

Both sides refusing to give in to make these wars end...

Unrest, Protest, has kept this part of the world aflame...

Blood of those who called themselves martyrs, blood of innocent children, only make Satan smile...

Arab Blood, Jewish Blood, can't find love for each other...

Tension all around, Peace nowhere to be found...

Venom in the heart, vengeance on the lips of many...

Weeping mothers, little children taught how to defend instead of how to befriend their neighbors.

Rock throwing against rapid-fire guns keeps Peace on the run... Missiles being prepped to devastate, and strong enough to annihilate...

Unity unable to get started with so many places being bombarded...

U.S. Intervention, Friend or Foe? Both sides want to really know?

Peacemakers or Nation Breakers?

Jerusalem a divided city... Our Land! Our Sacred Place! Both sides cry, leaving no place for compromise, while the prophets weep in their resting place....

BLACK HANDS

BLACK HANDS Started Civilization…

BLACK HANDS Built Civilizations…

We are a Powerful   Nation…

More than a Crime Story, More than a Burden…

It All Started in Africa… Bones proved it…

Anthropologist proved it and Science proved it…

Study unaltered History and You will prove it….

The clock ticks... Here we go again, unjustified
shootings of unarmed men and women of color.

– Word Bird

22

THE CLOCK TICKS

The clock ticks... Teach the children even if they don't belong to you...

The clock ticks... Rwanda, Darfur, Somalia blood tides on the rise, where is the global outcry?

The clock ticks... Death on the express route, coming unannounced, and leaving a trail of tears...

The clock ticks... It was written that "Every knee shall bow"... Riches won't save them, bowing to their own image won't save them...

The clock ticks... Here we go again, unjustified shootings of unarmed men and women of color.

The clock ticks... Hate breeding, Frighten adults and broken families on a global basis, affecting the growth of all nations...

The clock ticks... Hold on to the children... Evil is seeking them, bleeding them, afraid of them, for it was written that "A Child Shall Lead Them"...

The clock ticks... Chaos is the Flavor of the Month for too many months, and Poor People are not the only ones feeling the effects...

The clock ticks... The Waters are still poisoned in Flint and other places...

The clock ticks... Disorder in the Big White House

and the Signing of Bills, that were designed to Take back and Cutback vital and necessary programs, are on the rise again.

The clock ticks... Mother Earth is grieving again... More Tornado/ Hurricane sightings, more Waters Rising and the Mountains are Spewing Fire again...

Global Warming is God Yawning and hearing the cries of Mother Earth...

The clock ticks... Watch for the signs when God puts the twisted back in line, back in place, and save the human race...

No matter what is being done or said, GOD IS NOT DEAD...

Tick Tock... Tick Tock....

23

DO YOU KNOW ME?

My teachers were many: Jesus, Garvey, Elijah, Sojourner, Medgar, Harriet, Shaka, Malcolm, King...

Do You Know Me?

When I was little, the only accepted national theme song I ever heard was: "Get On Back if You Are Black," sung by a group called The Enforcers.

Do You Know Me?

I represent a tired majority who is always fighting for Dignity and Equality...

Do You Know Me?

I don't carry the American Express Card or have a fifty thousand dollar job, could that be the Reasons Why Life Is So Hard?

Do You Know Me?

I keep having these recurring images of the bottom of a ship, the sounds of a whip tearing into flesh, dark dungeons and screams that pierce the soul and make me tremble...

Do You Know Me?

My forefather was call Pharaoh my Mother was called Queen, they removed me from the Cradle of Civilization, made me build other Nations, gave me a

New Home called Plantations...

Do You Know Me?

They beat me until I Forgot my True Name, they
took all my clothing and replaced them with Chains...

Do You Know Me? Do You Know Me?

I sure as hell don't!

24

AFRICAN JESUS

African Jesus... In the Scriptures, in our Mind, even though others eyesight about YOU remains blind...

Blind to your Blackness, blind to the facts that everyone in your Birth Place started out Black...

African Jesus... We knew from how the Scriptures described your hair, your color, that you were an African Brother...

Your story was too powerful to ignore and they liked what they saw, so they gathered in Secret Quarters to start the Birth of New World Order...

They read about your deeds and how you brought the Devil to his knees, how you healed the sick, fed the poor and how you Rose from Death's door...

They altered the Scriptures and hid the rest, sat back and watched racism beat on its chest, while plotting to keep the Nations of Color oppressed...

African Jesus, our children are finding out that 'Hair like a Lamb and Burnt Feet, the Color of brass' not only represents the Sun/Son of Man, they are the features of a Blackman...

Pictures of the True You were kept from public view, they even had Michael Angelo, paint their European Version of You, (In Their Image)...

Beat that picture into our brain until we accepted the

change… We Hung White Jesus in our homes, in our churches, in our heart…

Prayed to White Jesus while your authentic picture gathered dust in vaults, in secret chambers, and basements.

Seeing you, in your unaltered form, has the Power to heal…

Seeing you, in the Image of a Blackman, has led to mass hysteria, mass cover-up, and the breaking up of lies that have been passed down for centuries…

Honor the Sun/Son of Man in His True Color…
Free your mind and stop being blind to the truth…

African Jesus… African Jesus, are you a believer or still a victim of the Great Deceiver? Asked yourself about yourself…

African Jesus… African Jesus…

If the Color of God doesn't matter, why was HIS diabolically changed?

Don't be afraid of the truth, there is always proof…

African Jesus… African Jesus…

See the Image in Your Mind and stop being blind.

25

WALKING PLANET

Planets in our solar system are beginning to realign themselves with other symbolic symbols that are known only to Ancient Time Keepers, who have been keeping a spiritual watch for centuries...

As if the formations were being guided by unseen ancient hands, we are in the midst of new, profound discoveries that are shaping and reshaping the destiny of man.

Scientist have often spoken about a Black-Hole that does not reveal what's inside of it...

Only the Ancient, who charted the sky and rode on the wings of the wind, know the purpose of these Black-Holes because they are spiritually connected to the soul of man and his existence...

Eons ago, this world was one of many that our ancestors spoke about, left records about, left symbols to verify their vast knowledge of things known only to them...

Left a legacy of truth that would one day realign itself with the stars and shine forth on Earth, giving birth to a Star Child, which would bring the Soul of Mankind home...

There are no new planets, according to the Ancient, because the Black man is a Walking Planet who has been taken out of his orbit and made to roam the galaxy living someone else's reality...

Because of who you really are, your future is aligned with the stars...

You are a Walking Planet... The day you truly understand this is the day of True Freedom for you...

The truth is in your Soul, Summon it to the Surface, You do have the Power...

You are a Walking Planet...

Scientist and others are still trying to find out your beginning on the Earth... You pre-date every known bone that they have discovered...

Your history began eons ago when the galaxy was being formed...

You are a Walking Planet, you were the first ones who lived among the stars...

Your true history is drenched in antiquity...

Search the Black-Hole of your Mind because in that darkness, the light of truth is waiting to grow...

You are a Walking Planet!

26

BLACK WOMAN

Do you really know how Beautiful you are?

Black Woman, you were born majestic and you were selected by the Creator to be a shining example of beauty at its Highest Peak...

Do you know, Black Woman, that you possess a strength that others admire?

Even if they don't confess, they know that You Are The Best.

Black Woman, Mother Earth, for centuries you have proven over and over again that there is no one quite like you.

Do you know, Black Woman. that the word Queen came from you when your presence first came into existence?

You have managed to hold your family together during difficult times, no female in history has taken as much abuse as you.

How you were able to keep your beauty in tact when everybody was trying to tear you down, remake you, taste and break you, shows the Strength that seeps through your pores.

Do you know, Black Woman, that the background is not the grounds you should be accustomed to?

When I see you, wherever I see you, Please Walk Proud, Look Proud, keep Your Beauty beaming above the crowd…

You Represent Beauty and Strength, take time to notice because I did.

This is my Tribute to You, Black Woman, No matter which Shade that Dominates Your Face, You bring so much Beauty to Our Race…

The First Woman, The First Queen, and the First to give Birth on The Earth, are titles that belong to you, Black Woman…

May these words find you and remind you of Who You Really Are…

Born to be a Star!

27

COMMUNICATORS

The Eyes spoke volumes even though a word was never uttered...

The tension filled the air with Cupid's tears...

Another garden growing dead because Love was not being properly fed...

Another of his precious arrows got uprooted and polluted...

The Eyes spoke volumes... They were distant, they seemed drained and filled with pain.

There was no laughter, and Church Hugs had Replaced Closeness.

Smiles were being sent out of the vicinity and warned not to come back.

Silence was given a New Role and Control of the atmosphere.

Conversations were regulated to nods and gestures that are filled with empty symbols and words that don't nurture the heart.

It is in the Eyes, where pools of emotions meet and can speak volumes...
without uttering a word.

Discover that you are not so bad after all
and when the confusion in your life clears,
you will still stand tall...

– Word Bird

28
IMAGE OF GOD

It is up to You to Prove Them All Wrong...

You were created in the Imago Dei (Image of God).

You owe it to yourself to Rise above all situations that are trying to hinder your growth.

It doesn't matter where you live, how you have been living, what you have done, or who you did it too...

You were created in the Imago Dei; take a little time and discover the Beauty of You...

Discover that you are not so bad after all and when the confusion in your life clears, you will still stand tall...

Image of God... No matter your race, your beliefs, your accent or how you are perceived by others, nothing or no one can take that fact away.

Search the scriptures, read the old text, God in His Infinite Wisdom created You in His Image to remind you of your greatness...

Remind You that regardless of your finances, regardless of your status and the reality that you are living, inside your mirror is His Image.

Doesn't matter the shape of your nose, or the size of your lips, or texture of your hair...

If you have Black Skin, Brown Skin, Light Skin, Red Skin, Yellow skin...

If you are Male or Female, Rich or Poor...

The Imago Dei is all on your face!

Always honor yourself for you are Representing The Creator.

Image of God... See it in the faces of the children... Embrace them, protect them, allow them to grow in the Resurrected Power and they will fulfill the Prophecy and Save Mankind.

Imago Dei is in You... How Are You Representing This Gift?

29

LEFT IN STONES

In Kemet, In Ethiopia, in Nubia, Benin and every other place on the Mother Continent, there is proof under all that pillage, decimation and devastation of those ancient nations, that Africa produced the First People on the Planet...

Left in Stones, Carved in Stones is the True History of an Ancient People whose descendants have been told Lies that have survived the many shifts of time...

Lies that suppressed the truth, and hid the truth about Africa's Place in history...

Lies that led to stealing of Ancient Cultures that were so magnificent that the Invaders raided and stole the identity, and made it their own...

Left in Stones, Carved in stones, by Ancient Planners who left monuments as records of their greatness, records of their existence...

Monuments and Structures that show a Mastery of Physics, Technology, Mathematics, that has often been imitated, but never truly duplicated...

We are an Ancient People no matter what is being told in these times, no matter what the altered and new written books say, the Pyramids are proof, the written History carved in the stones of ancient structures are proof...

Stolen Legacy led to a false claiming of ancient places, ancient glory that belonged to the people of that area, the people of that time...

Stolen legacy produced a new religion and forced the people away from spirituality and worshipping the Gods and Goddesses of their ancestors...

Stolen legacy began the destruction of artifacts and structures that resembled the original people of that time period...

Left in stones, Carved in stones are the written history of an ancient people whose descendants have been perpetually lied to...

Do the Research and Reverse the Curse... Meditate and see the images in your mind...

Left in Stones, Carved in Stones... Proof that the tomb robbers could not dilute.

HONOR THE ANCESTORS

I Know Not All the Names of The Gods and Goddesses, of My Ancestors, Nor the Symbols that Represent them, or the rituals to summon them...

I know not how to worship them, nor how to pronounce their names correctly...

Still, acknowledging them has always been Second Nature to me...

Acknowledging them because I always knew that books can be altered, re-printed and fitted to fill a need or greed, and to deceive...

Behold the Ancient Symbols of the Past, where each is a story within a story...

Divine Protection is the Only True Protection...

Honor The Ancestors in Your Heart, in Your Soul, even if you Know Them Not...

They Walk with You, Some were sent to Guide and Protect you...

Acknowledge the spirits within and find your power.

Let every drink that touch your lips be a libation for them.

FIRE IN YOU

There is a Fire in You, Black Woman, that yearns to be free...

Hot like the Sun, waiting to show everyone just how far you have come in reclaiming your rightful place as the first woman to have walked the earth...

I hear its Flames in your speech as the glow of your evolution continues towards its peak...

There is a Fire in you, waiting and anticipating your awakening....

Making its presence felt in your walk, in the clothes that you wear, which always bring out envy and lustful stares...

Your beauty, your charm and your alluring physical attractions has been known to run kings off their thrones and men away from their homes...

There is a Fire in you Black Woman... Felt it, seen it, got too close to it when you got upset and had to speed up my steps...

Fire came out the words of Nikki G., Maya, and Sonia Sanchez too... The Fire lives inside each of you...

Find Your Fire Queen of the Nile, none can match your tantalizing Style.

WHERE IS JUSTICE?

Does anyone know how and why Justice keeps avoiding those who really need it?

What Strong Forces are at work and so powerful that they can influence and make Justice do a disappearing act?

Where is Justice? Has anyone seen it visiting in the Poor neighborhoods?

Poor People have put out a Missing Person's Report in hopes of finding out what happened to Justice.

Where does Justice go when a crime has been committed against someone who can't afford a High-Price-Lawyer, who does not come from a Wealthy Family?

The people are getting tired of Marching, Screaming, Protesting and Rioting in search of Justice.

Where are the intense investigations that others receive when a crime has been committed against them?

Why can't poor, decent people penetrate the Blue Wall that often accompanies Police Brutality?

Why is it that the Media, the Politicians and Others who have the power to force Justice to show up, turn a deaf ear to the cries of a parent, a child, a mate, who is in desperate need of answers to stop their pain?

Where is Justice? Tell him to visit others, who for centuries have not been able to keep up with him.

Tell him we forgive him for hiding.

We know that he has been persuaded to keep a LOW and NO SHOW PROFILE for those who really need him.

Where is Justice? If you see him, hold him… Many people are convinced that he doesn't exist for them.

Where is Justice? Where is Justice?

On the Lips and Hearts of Black people…

On the Lips and Hearts of Latinos...

On the Lips and Hearts of Native Americans...

On the Lips and Hearts of White People, who Stand for Truth no matter the consequences or alienation that follows.

If you see Justice, tell him it's okay to stay.

Tell him we forgive him, just make his Presence Felt.

33

PROUD RACE

We are a Proud Race that is saturated in Antiquity...

A Race that has withstood Enslavement...

A Race that has been separated from its African Past...

A Race that has been divided, persuaded to fight amongst itself...

A Race that Started Civilization on its Path...

We are a Proud, Ancient Race that others claimed had no history worth talking about...

Your History is Not the History of Slaves...

Your History began in the Alpha...

We are a Proud Race of people whose natural kindness led to their enslavement...

We have been labeled wrong, judged wrong, conditioned to be dependent on someone else for Strength...

We are a Proud Race of Star Gazers, Nation Builders, who must reach out to those of us who been separated from the truth...

We are a Beautiful Race of People...

Look at our Females, see the Beauty and Strength

they possess in abundance...

Look at their Glow more brilliant than a Five Star Show when allowed to grow...

Look at the Men, even though the residue of slavery weaken many of them, you can still see the Ancestral Strength flowing and circulating throughout their bodies...

We are a Proud Race... The First Race to Represent the Human Race...

The Bones proved it, Pyramids, Ancient Structures throughout the Planet Proved it; and...

When Truth is Told Whole, that will Prove it!

34

DANCE BLACKMAN DANCE

Graceful Warriors take the stage, fill the aisles; the crowd shouts as the dancers come out...

Dance Blackman Dance...

Determined eyes, immense pride, graceful steps, what will these brothers do next?

Dance Blackman Dance...

Music is intoxicating, smiles are all around as the brothers are getting down.

Dance Blackman Dance...

Perfect blend of real black men, doing their steps while projecting dignity and respect...

Men of all ages, grace the stage and are not afraid to show a skill that many men won't reveal.

Dance Blackman Dance...

The sisters sit in awe and in glee at the strength and grace they see, while the brothers turn it up a notch and the place begins to rock.

Dance Blackman Dance...

Do it for the children, do it for the women, and do it for yourself, because inside you is an ocean of talent that you have never tapped into.

Dance Blackman Dance…

Do it for Sankofa, do it for the Maafa, and do it to commemorate the fact that you were born great.

Dance Blackman Dance…

Your joy is showing, your face is glowing, the Ancestors are dancing inside you and with you…

Dance in unity, dance in the spirit, dance with a purpose, just Dance Blackman Dance.

35

BLOODY HANDS

The Blood of My People is on Your Hands...

The Destiny of My People was altered by Your
Hands...

You-Know-Who-You-Are...

The Land of My People was taken and Raped
by Your Hands...

The Rivers of Blood were given Birth by Your
Hands...

You-Know-Who-You-Are...

The Spirit of My People Could Not Be Crushed
By Your Hands...

You are not nameless or blameless in the
Massacre of Countless Generations of My People.

You-Know-Who-You-Are: Devil Star...

Wicked, Vicious, Malicious, and You Find
Eating My People Alive Delicious...

You-Know-Who-You-Are... Your Hands drip
with the blood of My People who fought you,
resisted you, condemned you, exposed you
for the Fiend and Killer of Dreams that You are...

You –Know-Who-You-Are...

I Am Here to Expose You...

Wicked, Vicious, Malicious,
You Find Eating My People Alive
Delicious...

You Know Who You Are.

36

MAMA'S EYES

Through Mama's Eyes, I have looked and judged
you...

Her anger became my anger and your agony.

Through Mama's Eyes, I judged you like she did,
like society did, and all those others
who didn't understand you did...

Through Mama's Eyes, I saw all your faults
because she lost respect for you and showed me
how to too.

Your insecurities, your fears, could not be
shared with the family, for so much is always
expected out of you.

No one wants to talk about the Responsible
You, the Provider You, and the Warrior You...

No one wants to talk about how you paid the
bills, put food on the table, clothes on the back
of your children.

Everybody seems to have an opinion about
your behavior, your commitment, and
your love for your family.

This is for those fathers who are tired
of hearing how they never do enough
or did enough for their children and family.

Your stories have been left out, never talked
about for too long in any discussion.

Your love has always been strong, even if you
had to leave, you never took your Heart with you.

You never stopped loving your children,
regardless if they were kept from your vital input
and guidance.

In house fighting couldn't stop you, outside
pressure couldn't stop you from taking care of
your responsibilities...

Society won't clap for you, your children and
mate might not stand for you; still, in your heart,
you know you have tried to do your part.

This poem is for you fathers, who would not let
others define you...

In Mama's Eyes you didn't fight, you only took
flight....

37

WHEN THE BLACK WOMAN WEEPS

When the Black Woman weeps, the rivers speak
for it knows her pain lies deep...

All during her years , she has often been
the victim of countless tears.

She has often been misused and abused,
by her man, by The Man and by others
who just don't understand.

When the Black Woman Weeps, It Is Not
Because She Is Weak, It Is Because Her Pain
Lies River Deep...

Her pain she can no longer keep and letting the tears
flow is the only way she knows...

Weeping doesn't mean weak, it's the heart trying to
speak....

The videos don't lie, the cameras don't lie...
Eyewitnesses didn't lie....

– Word Bird

38

BLACK LIVES MATTER

These words are not a battle cry, not a call to Arms, they are just an accumulation of frustrations that have plagued Black People for centuries...

These words are not meant to incite, pick a fight with someone white...

They are a reminder to the racists, a reminder to people who cling to old beliefs and ideas about how to deal with and treat Black people...

As of words, the death count by the hands of the these police and those disturbed others, has reached epidemic proportions...

The videos don't lie, the cameras don't lie... Eyewitnesses didn't lie...

Black Lives Matter... Black Lives Matter...

Outcries from Racist in High and Low places are in an uproar because of the Marches and protests that are taking place, in every place where someone's family member has been killed unjustly...

Hiding behind the White Sheets is no longer a concern of those who still view Black People in disgust and mistrust...

Blaming the victims for their own demise is giving top priorities and guarded by a Blue Wall of Silence and Violence...

Getting off without penalties has become almost the norm for those who wish Black people had never been born...

For those who can't hide the hate, can't hide the feelings to regulate and subjugate and devastate anyone not the Right Color in their racist eyes...

The Marches say, "We are tired of revolving Courts, that are not in favor of the victims...

"We are tired of blatant Police Brutality going unpunished...

"Tired of being seen as 3/5 a people"... The Marches say, "Enough of this Shi...t,

"Enough of losing a loved one who did nothing wrong...

"Enough of the guilty smirking and getting desk duties with pay until they can retire and fade away...

"Enough of weeping parents, children, husbands and wives, whose eyes can't hide the pain they constantly feel on their inside"...

The blood money doesn't take their pain away, the Marches and protests don't take the pain away... Time doesn't take the pain away...

Black Lives Matter... Black Lives Matter...

If these words are upsetting to some, too damn bad! Black people are tired of being the only ones frustrated and sad...

We Standing up, Getting up, Waking up, and We are Fed up!

39

VERDICT

Again, we are in disbelief at a clear cut Verdict...

Again, we shed a tear, voice our anger, while the Devil smiles...

Again we watch a parent scream in agony over the dismissal and twice killing of their child...

They know in their soul that lies were told...

Wallet 'gun' in their reports, resisting arrest in their reports, suspicious-acting- behavior in their reports, and any other word that can be used to justify a crime is in their reports...

"How Long Lord?" Screamed the multitudes who know in their heart that wrong is wrong and THIS, like so many other Verdicts, is wrong...

People are tired of hearing "Proper Procedures" when their loved ones are innocent of all charges, and the guilty go free to fade away from public view and opinions...

People are tired of hearing about blood payoffs to families that can never replace a lost loved one.

It rained that day; heaven, as if on cue, opened up the gates to show its disgust with man's version of justice.

Mini-rioting, sprouting all over the inner cities...

Police prepared for chaos and unrest...

Again, we are left with anger; again, another innocent person is dead; and again, justice is a no show.

Too many Verdicts favor those who should be punished...

Too many Verdicts are openly wrong in their decisions by peers that look nothing like the accused, by Laws and Racist attitudes which dominate the jury, even before the trial.

Not Guilty! even when the seeing Camera/ Video was present...

Not Guilty! even when no weapons, drugs, found on the suspect...

Not Guilty! even with Hands in the Air, or up against a Wall...

Not Guilty! even when the evidence shows out-of-control behavior, excessive force, and no justifiable reason for stoppage...

Soon this Verdict, like all the other unjustifiable Verdicts, will be taken out the Press, while Racism rests and beats on its chest...

Open Your Eyes as Well as Your Mind... Say Something!

40

JUSTICE OR ELSE

The people are coming:

It was in their eyes... Fire... Anger... Determination to shake up this Nation...

Every footstep was a testimony of Unified Strength, walking towards a Common goal of being heard, being Seen...

They were tired of Living a Nightmare and wanted one of the Dreams of Martin Luther King to become a reality in their lifetime...

Their eyes carried the Fire and the Spirits of the Unjust, of the Victims of Brutality and Senseless Crimes that boggled the mind...

Their faces didn't come to entertain, they came to break some chains that should have long ago been broken, to break some traditions that led to some of these dreadful conditions...

They came to express their Unified Feelings about Justice or Else!

They came to send a Unified message that Change is needed now... Not Tomorrow, Not Later, NOW!

Walking with the blessings of their Ancestors in every step, with the Blessing of every victim that didn't make a headline, didn't make the news...

This time, Justice or Else had a Unified Voice, a United Voice that was tired of Promises that were never going to be fulfilled…

Tired of Waiting for God-Given-Rights to be given also to them…

This time, Justice or Else stood out like a wave and the Eyes of the World would take notice…

This time, the Fires of discontent would be given Center Stage and allowed to express the grievances, the disdain and anger of the people.

Justice or Else! Said the Red Nation….

Justice or Else! Said the Black and Brown Nations…

Justice or Else! Said the Oppressed, the Victims of Brutality, the Invisible Nations within this Nation…

The People are coming and this time the War Cry will be unified as the oppressed tribes of Humanity take Center Stage, and they are not afraid…

Justice or Else! So much more than a Slogan…

As of these words, some of the Children of tomorrow have decided to take matters in their own hands….

41

REALM OF THE MOMENT

Sometimes, even I have to be reminded of 'Who-I-Am' and 'Who-Is-Guiding Me' All this time...

Reminded that Current Situations are Trial Laced Situations that I will survive...

The Devil Truly is a Liar and will never make me a Member of His Choir...

I Shall be the One To Uplift the Mind, Heart, and Personal Life of Those who Stood by me, assisted me, cared for me, and loved me through it all...

I shall take control of the helm and stir My Life Ships to Safe Waters, a Safe Haven...

God Always takes care of His Birds...

My Time is Soon Time, Watch my Shine,

Watch my Glow, Watch my Flow and watch me Grow...

My Time is Soon Time...

Elevation is near, Life Starter Kit is within Reach...

God operates in the Realm of The Moment.

It is here where all my Personal Fears will Disappear...

It is here where Pretend Strength will be Replaced with Real Strength…

It is here where the Heart will find Solace and a Resting Place…

In The Realm of The Moment, Financial Blessings shall sprout like Flowers watered often by heavenly rain…

In The Realm of The Moment, Health Matters won't matter for the Spirit and Body is Renewed… The Mind and the Soul is Rejuvenated and seeks to Soar Once More…

In The Realm of The Moment, Blessings from Out-of-The-Blue will keep coming at you…

Patience, Faith, and Unyielding Convictions and Beliefs that Your Steps are Ordered Steps that have been Blessed, will keep you going and growing…

Yesterday grief can easily turn into Tomorrow's Peace in The Realm of The Moment…

Continue to Believe and Wait to Receive.

42

D-I-A-L

Come Travel with Me to a place of Peace and Tranquility.

A place that is always near but can take you far beyond your wildest dreams.

Come and get refocused and away from all these silly notions that there is No Peace On Earth.

There is a number that you can call anytime or anyplace, All you have to do is Dial 1-800-My-Mind.

You are born equipped with this number. Stop Hanging Up on Yourself! The number is Toll-Free.

When everything around you brings you to the point of depression, Dial The Number...

When Stress tries to overtake you... Dial The Number...

When no one seems to understands or give-a-damn, Dial The Number...

Before you reach a Breaking Point and do harm to self or others... Dial The Number...

Please note that when 1-800-My-Mind seems to have a Busy Signal or you can't seem to get through, try calling out the Name Jesus while waiting, He's been known to always answer the phone.

Your words came out in trembles, yet There You Stood, talking while weeping as if the tears were invisible to the naked eyes…

– Word Bird

43

THERE YOU STOOD

Just for a Moment, I Saw you and Through you...

There You Stood like a Rock with tears in your eyes that began to swell and overflow on the floor, like rain drops, and you couldn't stop...

There You Stood feeling helpless, feeling dejected and rejected in their eyes, in your own eyes...

There You Stood in weepiness because another Holiday is coming, a Holiday of Giving, and the thoughts brought out grief instead of euphoria...

On the inside you wept and only you and God saw this...

On the outside the masks were beginning to break down because of all the erosion being caused by the recent surges of troubled waters near your heart...

There You Stood surrounded by an Aura of Pretend Calmness, Pretend Togetherness, while tightening your Armor of Pretend Emotions...

Just for a moment the shield was lifted from the fog you had maintained throughout your life...

Slipping in to darkness no longer worked and your eyes were revealing your hurt...

Your words came out in trembles, yet There You Stood, talking while weeping as if the tears were invisible to the naked eyes...

Standing like a Mountain, while Weeping Inside like a Fountain…

I Saw You because Once, I Was You…

Come out of the Shadows and rejuvenate your self-esteem, so that you can catch up with your dreams…

There You Stood Standing like a Mountain, while Weeping inside like a Fountain.

44

HUMAN FOUNTAIN

There is a Fountain of great, useful ideas inside of You...

Your mannerism, your quiet fire is the envy of many...

Your inner and outer beauty also can stir conversations.

You are loved by family and friends...

Words like 'Dedicated Friend' and 'Dedicated Educator' have no problems being attached to you...

Students love the way you treat them, teach them and try to reach them...

They know; they see that caring comes easy for you, that understanding their life and plight comes easy for you...

You are a Fountain of untapped possibilities, and what you bring to the table of education has always been about feeding the needs of the children.

I applaud you because I see the joy in many of their eyes when it concerns you...

I applaud you for not backing down when others try to shift your Natural Born Crown.

These words are just a poetic reminder to keep climbing, _____.

Keep climbing...

This system needs your fire; this system needs an injection of your caring nature...

This system needs you in high places, reaching those trapped in stagnation, and non-productivity.

Your Fountain will bring out the hate; your fountain will bring out the great...

Keep on being you; those test, those who want to bring you stress, will wither and fade because there is fire in you and a Fountain that refuses to be denied...

You understand when others might not give-a-damn!

45

SUCCESSFUL LOVE

The Fire in a relationship must Always Stay Lit…

Love is such a demanding emotion, it seeks Total Devotion.

When you are Lucky enough to capture a True Love, then Cherish it, Caress it, and don't take advantage of it.

Don't look for excuses to dilute it, Love is like the four seasons; it doesn't need much of an excuse to seek change.

Love is Selfish; It requires your Full Attention…

The Flames of love must always stay lit or love will depart and once again leave you with a broken heart.

Too many people forget the little things that made love come to them.

Too many people try to Buy Love when Love is Priceless…

Too many people try to love 'More Than One' when love is all about Oneness.

A Successful Love won't turn its back on you, for it seeks to become a Permanent Part of You…

If you want your love to last and not become a thing of the past, Keep it Strong… Keep it Strong…

Many have tried to keep love alive, but only the True Strong can Survive...

Sometimes, saying the words "I-Love-You" is Not Enough to keep a good thing from turning into dust.

A Successful Love depends on Both of You to keep each other always feeling new.

Keep it Strong... Keep it Strong...

It Will Be Tested.

46

YOUTH AGAINST YOUTH

In Some neighborhoods, The Violence Against Each Other has Reached Epidemic Proportions.

Bullets flying over a Diss, Robbery for a Coat, a Watch, some Jewelry, a Stare...

Gang Activity Overflowing In Some Neighborhoods...

Angry young men and young ladies roam the streets, the subways, in search of victims who they can overpower, frighten, and introduce to the Elements of Hurt and Fear.

Another funeral, another family weeps... Hanging sneakers, colorful murals, disbelieving lips and Angry, Vengeful eyes follow the processions to the grave.

Talks of Payback and Revenge keep the undertakers busy...

Stabbings, Shootings, daily intake for many of our young people, who have become callous, conditioned to the Violence Against Each Other.

Wrong Colors Set Them Off, Wrong Clothes has led to Gun Fire...

Wrong Choices have led many of Them to Prison or the Grave.

The gunmen are getting younger and younger. The victims are coming from every household, even those who have control of their children.

Stray bullets ring through the night and day, Killing and Wounding Innocence...

Rap Wars, Street Wars, Keeps the Flames of Pain Burning continuously...

Too many funerals for Young People, too much violence against each other. Not Enough Positive Role Models for Them to Follow.

Our Young People are dying in Record Numbers because of their inability to maintain Respect for Each Other.

"Stop The Violence!" has to become More than a Slogan if we are going to Save This Generation of Young People...

We must find a way to remove the bitterness, the disappointments and the anger that has become the norm for so Many of Them.

Youth Against Youth. The Violence is Overflowing

13... Life is Gone... 14... Life is Gone... 15... Life is Gone... On and On, the Numbers Increase while Our Heart continues to weep.

Young People, Please Take Heed or This Generation will Continue to Bleed Away its Future...

13... Life is Gone... 14... Life is Gone... 15... Life is Gone... On and On, the Numbers Increase, while

Loved Ones continue to Weep, and the Death Angel continues to make its presence felt...

Youth Against Youth, Tired of the Headlines that Boggles the Mind...

Losing too many to the streets, to gun fire and bad attitudes.

The Gathering Came With Divine Blessings,
and The Men Stood Like Mountains,
and called His Holy Name.

– Word Bird

47

THE GATHERING

The Brothers came with a purpose, written in every step, every face...

It was Scriptural, It was Spiritual...

The men came from All Walks of Life...

Came because it was written that "They would gather in His Holy Name."

Each handshake, each embrace tore down walls of indifference, stirred memories of a Million Men, and made the Ancestors smile.

Positive energy permeates this place... GOD is in this place.

You can see the traces of Him in their beaming faces.

Hear it in their Voices, as the men say:

> "We Are The Men Of God!
> See Him In Us...

> "We Are The Men Of God!
> Pray With Us...

> "We Are The Men Of God!
> Living Testimonies of His Resurrection Power.

"We Are The Men Of God!
Protected And Selected.

The Imago-Dei Cannot Be Denied,
It Is In Our Eyes...
See It In Our Dance,
Hear It In Our Voices...

The Gathering Came With Divine Blessings, and
The Men Stood Like Mountains, and called His
Holy Name...

Clap Your Hands For Jesus and give your
neighbor a hug, for The God We Serve Is All
About Love!

48

IF THEY KNEW

You could see the pain in so many faces...
People of every race shook their heads in disbelief as
the Twins came tumbling down...

Frantic search for the missing went around the
clocks non-stop...

The scent of Death was everywhere along with
The countless tears...

They say the government knew that death was
near and didn't warn all its citizens...

They say messages were passed to and from
careless hands and indecisive minds, who knew
that death was going to make a mass appearance
on American soil.

They say most of the terrorist were trained with
America's help and finances... Trained to fly, and
trained to bomb, and cause a lot of harm to a
lot of people...

If the government knew, why couldn't they tell
people like me and you?

Why did the warning if imminent danger only
reach certain sects and not us all?

No one told the majority of the American
people to stay away on that fatal day...

If the government knew, why wasn't it in the Newspapers, on television screens, on the radio?

So many lost lives... never to be found...

All those body parts left behind to remind us that War is hell and sometimes the innocent pays...

There will never be closure because every time there is a breeze blowing, fragments of 911 blows with it...

Pieces of someone's loved one will forever circulate in the air, as a painful reminder of 911...

listen to the winds, hear the calls of innocence... Ashes to Ashes, Dust to Dust, Now we must wait for J-U-S-T-I-C-E...

We who lead other nations in technological advancement, and can send men into space and beyond, why is it so difficult to find Ben Laden and company, unless we have also taught them the art of invisibility?

If they knew, do you really think they would tell you?

So many questions, so little answers, every agency is blaming each other while the families of innocence suffer...

Monetary gains won't stop the pain, ease the tears, or fill out the missing years of someone you love...

If they knew, may every night when they close their eyes be a nightmare...

We will never forget because every time the wind blows an Innocent soul blows with it.

It took a killer wave to get people's attention
that even paradise can be disturbed when
God Gives The Word...

– Word Bird

49

THE EARTH SHOOK

And the Earth Shook... The serene waters became hands and reached out and covered the land...

Everything in its path was altered, uprooted and scattered in the waters, which seemed to be everywhere...

Utopia for many had become a death pool; Missing children, missing loved ones all were claimed by the waters...

Without warning the waters came and no science, no technology could prevent the earth from exhaling and shaking...

The outcries, the wailing, and the destruction made the world take notice...

So many bodies... so many bodies in the aftermath...

It took a killer wave to get people's attention that even paradise can be disturbed when God Gives The Word...

Tsunamis, Mudslides, Hurricanes and Wind, Weather Changes All Over The Globe.

Our Creator is not pleased and people need to start taking heed and hear the cries of humanity.

It was written that "Every Knee Would Bow"...

How many more signs, Mankind, will it take to get you Awake or must the Earth Once Again Shake?

When God searches your heart, will his Tears Start?

50

THIS GENERATION

They are not singing songs like, "WE SHALL OVERCOME"…

They are not afraid of police or guns…

In some inner cities, young people have gathered like a swarm of angry bees, joining the Marches, joining the Protests, and in some cases, leading the Marches and Protests…

Leading with a rock in hand, a mask on face, not afraid to confront and start a fire, start a riot, to express their contempt for injustices that have reached their neighborhoods, their loved ones or friends.

This Generation is Not like Past Generations…

More sullen, more likely to fight back and Clap back, even when not pushed…

Underneath that Sag and Swag is a generation like a Molotov cocktail, a mixture of brilliance, cocky, rude, stubborn, confused, angry and explosive…

All created from the frustrations, injustices and tolerance of their forbearers…

Unbeknown to many of them is that they carry the

spirits of the Ancestors who fought on the Ships, fought on the Plantations, and fought anywhere their life was being compromised or threatened…

Many of them carry the spirit of warriors, known and unknown, inside of them waiting to be activated and elevated to a new destiny…

Waiting to be stirred to a current awareness that requires putting down the weed and other drugs, leaving the gangs behind and getting in line with the rest who came to Protest.

Many of them see Trayvon in themselves, saw the videos and read the reports about the violence and murders against other Men of Color…

Many of them have seen the violence, up close and personal, against each other, against those who sported the wrong colors in their confrontational eyes…

Many of them finally heard the cries and realized that Black Lives Do Matter and these Marches, these Protests need their input, need their anger and determination to keep surging when the elders are tired; keep fighting for the things that were promised to everyone in this country.

It was written in the Great Book that "A Child Shall Lead Them"…

This Generation is Not like Past Generations... Be leery because they can be scary.

Still Growing to the tune of
"Ain't No Stopping Me Now"...

– Word Bird

51

STILL GROWING

When doubt is laced in your conversation when it concerns me, please reach for this and read this over and over again until these words sinks in...

I am not a new creation just an improved creation...

I live to love and be loved...

I seek to hold on, stay with and always treasure you who carry my heart...

I am no longer untrustworthy, unfaithful, and unsure of what I want in life...

Search not for the old me for that person no longer exists...

That person has been laid to rest and he who stands before you is highly blessed...

I stand anew in God's eyes long before it will reach your eyes...

I stand anew and I am true to my God as I am to you...

I stand anew and don't be startled and suspicious of my glow, it's just God you know.

Look at me with your heart instead of your eyes;
Envy free is what I be, truly I am not the enemy; I am not a threat, I am someone who just wants respect.

My conscious is clear just like my words; and if you must judge me, let my words represent me in the courtroom of your soul.

Still Growing to the tune of "Ain't No Stopping Me Now"...

Still Growing like a fresh planted tree...

Like the Sun rising over the Horizon...

Regardless of past mistakes, regardless of mating with procrastination, and chasing the wrong dreams...

Still Growing, and this time, I am leaving behind negative energy, and people who don't believe in themselves or in me.

Search not for the old me, for that person no longer exists and I thank God for this...

Got to keep going because I am Still Growing, and I can't grow standing still...

Feel me because this is the "Real Me".

52

LIKE YOU

I have seen the Waters, Quiet like you, Vibrant like you, Rise to new heights like you...

Seen the Waters flow with grace like you, mind its own Life Given Business like you, and rise to a crescendo like you...

Waves come out of you, Tornadoes too, even saw a flood of emotions come out of you...

I have seen the Waters soothe people like you do, mesmerize them like you always do, by just being you...

I have seen the Waters inside of you, felt their soothing depths as they took my heart to levels of pleasure that only my heart can measure...

Keep bathing me and saturating me in the comfort of your loving, oceanic heart...

Drowning in the name of love has never felt so good....

Scattered seeds... The Great African Tree continues to bleed for her lost children, who have been taught and conditioned to forget her....

– Word Bird

53

NEVER HEALED

The wounds have never healed...

The recurring nightmares and residue of slavery now haunts our children...

Haunts them in ways that manifest itself in their frustration and anger...

Haunts them where many of them don't care to hear about history... Don't care to hear about loving themselves above all else.

The wounds have never healed...

Slave mentality still a reality for many of the descendants of Africa...

Scattered seeds... The Great African Tree continues to bleed for her lost children, who have been taught and conditioned to forget her...

Our fears have not disappeared...

The MAAFA stories must continue to be told for generations to come...

The stories of Colonization... Enslavement... Castration of Black Men... Jim Crow and his legion... Rape of our women... Displacement of the

Black families... Willie Lynch and the White House
Pimps, must be told!

Our Wounds have not healed...

We must face the present with energy, vigor, and
teach our children to stop calling themselves
Nig@**s...

Teach the children, so that generation after generation
rediscovers that the strength of black people is like no
others...

The strength of Black People will always surface
during our darkest hour...

Scattered Seeds of Antiquity ... Survivors of a Black
Holocaust, your indomitable Spirit could never be
broken.

Our Wounds have not healed...

Our Tears have not stopped... Justice has not come
to folks who need it... Racism is still running amuck
and setting up shop in the Big White House...

Lost children of the Great African Tree, as long as
you remain apart from each other, disrespect each
other, not see the Imago-Dei in each other...

Our Wounds Will Never Heal!

Our children will continue the cycle of low
production and self-destruction...

Put aside the false pride, stop believing in the Keepers
of The Lie and

RISE...

           RISE...

                      RISE!

Respect for the elders shows respect toward God for
they led the way and are the beginning
seeds of our yesterdays.

– Word Bird

ABOUT THE AUTHOR

Malik Samuel Canty is a recognized retired Educator of the New York City Dept of Education, who served as a member of the United Federation of Teachers for 40 years. He is also an author of four additional books and a spiritual poet, who speaks for the voiceless. Known around the poetry circuit as the "Word Bird," Malik has performed in various places, including The Apollo Theatre, Brooklyn Academy of Music, The Schomburg Cultural Center, and as a Semi-Finalist in the McDonald's Gospelfest. Other venues, where his talents have been recognized, are: The World Poetry Convention, and several churches located in Harlem, Queens, Long Island, and repeatedly at the St. Paul Community and Mount Pisgah Baptist Churches in Brooklyn New York.

In addition, author Malik S. Canty has been published in various magazines and anthologies such as: Class Magazine, Afro Times newspaper and "Our World's Best Poet" anthology.

Word Bird writes to reveal the messages in his soul and as a witness of the durability of his people. The spirit and eyes of many speak to his soul, which lead him to intuitively write and speak for those individuals and groups, who are either afraid, who are incapable of expressing themselves, or who just don't know how to communicate effectively.

For more information, poetry, bookings or to simply connect with this prolific poet and author, visit the following platforms:

- **Email** – poeticwordbird@gmail.com

- **Poetry** –
  https://hubpages.com/@poeticwordbird

- **Website** – http://malikcanty.com

- **Facebook** –
  www.facebook.com/WordBirdthePoet
  https://www.facebook.com/wordthy1

- **Amazon Author Page** –
  https://www.amazon.com/Malik-
  Canty/e/B00JL6XK5Q